Kids & Computers

Virtual Reality & Beyond

Charles A. Jortberg

Published by Abdo & Daughters, 4940 Viking Drive, Suite 622, Edina, Minnesota 55435.

Copyright © 1997 by Abdo Consulting Group, Inc., Pentagon Tower, P.O. Box 36036, Minneapolis, Minnesota 55435 USA. International copyrights reserved in all countries. No part of this book may be reproduced in any form without written permission from the publisher.

Printed in the United States.

Cover and Interior Photo credits: Wide World Photos
                                     Archive Photos
                                     Jortberg Associates
                                     Super Stock
                                     Bettmann Archive

Edited by John Hamilton

Library of Congress Cataloging-in-Publication Data

Jortberg, Charles A.
   Virtual reality and beyond / Charles A. Jortberg.
   p. cm. -- (Kids and computers)
   Includes index.
Summary: Discusses virtual reality and other forms of computer simulation and examines their past, present, and future uses.
ISBN 1-56239-728-1
1. Computer simulation--Juvenile literature. 2. Virtual reality--Juvenile literature. [1. Virtual reality. 2. Computer simulation.] I. Title. II. Series: Jortberg, Charles A. Kids and computers.
QA76.9.C65J67 1997
006--dc20
                                           96-32641
                                                CIP
                                                AC

About the Author

Charles A. Jortberg graduated from Bowdoin College in 1951 with a Bachelor's Degree in Economics. Mr. Jortberg joined IBM in 1954 and served in several capacities. Among his assignments were coordinating all of IBM's efforts with the Air Force, managing a 20-person team of IBM engineers, and directing a number of technical programs at NASA's Electronic Research Laboratory. He formed Jortberg Associates in 1972, where he currently works, to provide an outlet for his start-up technology experience.

Contents

Virtual Reality and Beyond 4

Flight Simulators 7

The Weather Bureau 11

The Future 16

Computer Science Careers 24

    • Computer Design 25

    • Computer Manufacturing 26

    • Programming 27

    • Graphic Design 28

Glossary 29

Index 30

Virtual Reality and Beyond

For many years, large computers have been used to imitate a number of things. This imitation is known as "simulation." Some very large computer programs have been written to make the simulation as close to the real thing as possible. In today's language, this is known as "virtual reality."

Among the first uses of simulation was the training of pilots. An aircraft simulator is a small room shaped like an aircraft cockpit, or nose cone. Inside this room is an exact copy of the plane's instrument panel.

A flight student sits in a cockpit seat and goes through every action of "flying" the plane. The windshield of the simulator is actually a small computer screen that portrays the outside as it would appear from a real plane. The student's actions with the stick and rudders have the same effect as they would in reality.

Airplane takeoff performance-monitoring simulator.

The instrument panel of the simulator is also exactly the same as a real plane. All of this make-believe is made possible by a big computer that is attached to the model by wires and cables. The computer uses a complex program that sends signals to a collection of levers and gears that move the simulator as if it were flying. The computer also sends signals to the instruments in the simulator showing fuel, altitude, and all the other things a pilot needs to know.

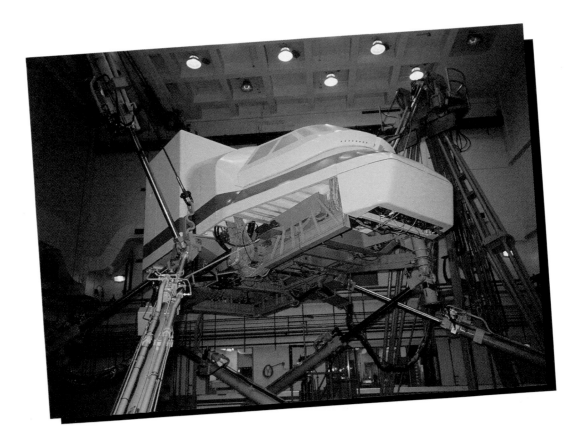

NASA's Space Shuttle flight simulator.

Flight Simulators

Flight simulators are now so realistic that major airlines train all of their pilots in them before they ever fly the real thing. Flight simulators are especially useful in training pilots for emergencies.

An instructor outside the simulator can cause the model of the plane to dive, or to lose one of its engines. It's a lot safer to train a pilot in the simulator than in a real plane with hundreds of passengers.

Another important use of computer simulation is in the space program. In the past, our astronauts have traveled millions of miles inside spacecraft simulators before they ever left the launching pad.

In the first moon mission, NASA built a complete model of the surface of the moon, including its rough terrain, to train the crew on landing techniques. These same crews were subjected to emergencies, such as seen in the movie "Apollo 13," in the simulator, and they were given grades on how they handled themselves. Simulation is still used to train space shuttle and

Voyager 2 on its approach to Uranus.

Saturn's ring system seen from *Voyager 2*.

future space station crews. Like airplane simulators, these spacecraft simulators are less expensive and a much less dangerous way to train astronauts.

Another form of virtual reality has been used very successfully by NASA in developing images from the millions of bits of data from their deep-space probes. For over 10 years, *Voyager 1* and *Voyager 2* have traveled deep into space to explore the planets Jupiter, Saturn, Uranus, and Neptune. These two rocket-driven space probes came within 25,000 miles of these planets and sent back radio signals that came from

A false-color image of Neptune, taken by *Voyager 2*.

hundreds of sensors on board. Radio signals were converted into numbers that described the planets from that altitude. NASA's huge computers took these millions of numbers and used them to produce the most startling images of the planets ever seen. Without this computer power it would have been impossible to create these images.

Another use of virtual skills is in the tracking of meteors done by NASA and the Smithsonian Institute in Washington, D.C. The two agencies have produced very accurate models of several meteors, and have drawn up a schedule of how close each will come to Earth.

The Weather Bureau

The U.S. Weather Bureau also makes extensive use of virtual reality. On some TV weather reports you will see the weather forecaster take you on a tour of the country showing what's happening in each region. In some regions you are taken through a rainstorm, or a snowstorm, and in others bright sunlight. These tours are computer generated from data inside the computers of the Weather Bureau.

For years airplanes have flown from Florida into the eyes of hurricanes. They have gathered millions of pieces of data about what makes up these killer storms, and are now using this data to create storm models. These models will be used to study new techniques in reducing the damage from hurricanes. They are also doing the same thing with tornadoes, but gathering information is difficult because you can't fly a plane into a tornado.

With the power and speed of the modern personal computer, the use of simulation and virtual reality is now being expanded to hundreds of new uses. In virtual reality computers can create

The Weather Bureau watches changing patterns in the weather via computer.

a model of a completely separate area from where you are. It is as if one minute you are seated in a chair in your house or your classroom, and when you put on a special helmet and gloves, you are transformed to a completely different place. In reality you haven't moved, but in virtual reality you have been transported to a whole new world, one that exists only inside the computer and in your mind.

In some virtual-reality systems, the computer is connected to your helmet and gloves. The experience is much different than looking at a television or computer display. Through its programs the computer creates another environment, and you're right in the middle of it. If it was just a television or computer screen, when you looked around you wouldn't see anything different. In the virtual environment you are totally relocated. As you move or turn your head, the computer changes the vision in your helmet and gives the impression of a completely different place or viewpoint.

With a specially wired glove you can feel as if you are actually touching or moving objects. The computer is really changing the image on your display to make it look as if you are making contact.

While the use of these devices has been widely adapted into some video games, future games will have the effect of transporting you completely to another location along with the appropriate sounds, smells, and sensations. Instead of just steering the wheel of a race car and looking at a picture of the

road, you will actually feel the motion of the car. When you turn your head you will see scenery whizzing by, and you will hear the wind and the roar of your engine. All of this will happen while you're still in your living room, or wherever your computer system is set up.

In addition to having great fun with virtual reality, it is also now being used in a number of businesses. General Motors and other companies have made good use of virtual reality in manufacturing cars to evaluate new interior and window designs. Companies planning new offices or factories have made extensive use of virtual reality by creating accurate models of the buildings. Employees can then try out the virtual buildings and give feedback.

Opposite page: A student from the Massachusetts Institute of Technology wears a virtual reality headset with a miniature camera in front of his eye. He transmits everything he sees onto the Internet.

The Future

With the rapid growth in the speed and uses of computers, the future promises to be truly exciting. The use of virtual reality will be expanded into areas not even thought of before. Imagine learning to drive a car by sitting at your computer. Instead of just looking at a picture of the road, you have the feeling of actually being in the car, with all the sights and sounds surrounding you. A program in the computer will put you into real-life situations, such as driving on a two-lane road and passing a truck, or parking the car in a really tight area. If you perform a task the wrong way, the computer simulates an accident. There might even be programs that will give you a driver's test to see if you're ready.

Other virtual reality programs will be available to take you into space, under the ocean, and into the center of the earth. For regions in the United States where kids have to travel many miles to school, there might be computer programs that let them stay at home and still be an active part of a class, which may have other kids from all over the world.

This 11-year-old boy reacts to the visuals of a virtual reality game.

ICAADS WALKTHROUGH

New computer displays and programs will be available that will present lifelike images of people for the training of doctors. These "patients" will be operated on in virtual reality, and if the students make mistakes, they can see the results.

Police officers will be trained in very true-to-life situations, like routine traffic stops or bank robberies. They will be trained on what to do, and then graded on how well they did.

At large airports, control of air traffic will be even more computerized. All airplanes nearing the airport will have a display that will show detailed pictures of any planes that are near them, and will direct this traffic automatically.

There will be a new range of computers designed to talk with each other with radio and TV signals that will be hundreds of times faster than today's telephone lines. All of your classroom work will be available for you to review before exams by merely keying in the subject material. An entire year's worth of lectures could also be reviewed. If you needed to write a paper for school and couldn't get to a library, all you would have to do is speak to your computer and it would find the material you needed and either print it or display it on your screen.

Opposite page: Computers are being used in the design of office and warehouse space.

DeeDee Jonrowe talks to her mother during the fifth day of the Iditarod Trail Sled Dog Race, on a live video teleconference setup.

Going to school may never be the same. In the new classrooms there will be wide use of computer and video conferencing. One school may have all of the best science teachers, while another the best English program. Through the use of computer and video conferencing, all students in all schools will have the benefit of the best programs. With virtual reality programs, you will be able to perform laboratory experiments even though the "laboratory" is actually a creation of the computer program. Textbooks may gradually disappear as all the up-to-date information on any subject becomes available merely by speaking into your computer.

When it comes time to think about colleges, you can call up a particular school's World Wide Web page and tour the campus, as well as look at all the courses. You will also be able to have a computer/video conference with students to ask them about life on campus.

With interactive TV and your computer, you will be able to change the outcome of certain programs by giving your input by voice or keyboard. In sports events you will experience the reality of action in football and hockey as computer graphics show the path of the puck and the ball. The role of referees and umpires may slowly fade away as computers and special sensors measure the strike zone in baseball, and also give calls of safe or out at first base or at home. Tennis courts may someday be wired into computers that will give foolproof rulings on whether shots are in or out.

This computer student looks into the past with his virtual reality helmet.

On some high-speed roads, your car may be driven for you by automatic sensors in the road and a computer on your car. When you get in the car, you will tell the computer where you want to go, and the car will be guided to that destination by the computer. The sensors will make sure you avoid all other traffic and stay operating at safe speed. Of course, if there is a problem with the computer, you will still be able to operate the car as you do now.

Automobiles will be equipped with automatic collision detection sensors and computers. In these cars, if a collision is about to occur, the computer will sound an alarm and either brake, turn, or speed up to avoid the crash.

Most photography will be done with digital cameras that let you look at the results right away on your camera, your TV, or computer. You'll easily be able to alter the pictures to suit your tastes, such as making them smaller, larger, or different colors.

If you want to send copies of pictures to your friends in other parts of the world, all you'll have to do is send them from your computer by a modem or satellite uplink.

Computer Science Careers

There is nothing in the world that holds as much promise for future careers as computer-related fields. Every aspect of our future will depend heavily on some form of computer activity, either directly or indirectly. As this future continues to unfold, it is clear that hundreds of thousands of job opportunities will await those who are willing to work for it, and who are willing to use their imaginations. Some of these fields include the following:

Computer Design

Thousands of jobs will be filled in those companies that design and build computers and the devices they use. For many of the jobs you will need to be good at math and science. People in these jobs will also make good use of computers as they design the machines of the future.

Computer aided design/drafting program.

Computer Manufacturing

People will be needed to design and run the complicated automatic machines that manufacture the parts and pieces that make up the modern computer. Many of these jobs will be involved with the use of computers to automatically do the manufacturing, including the use of robots.

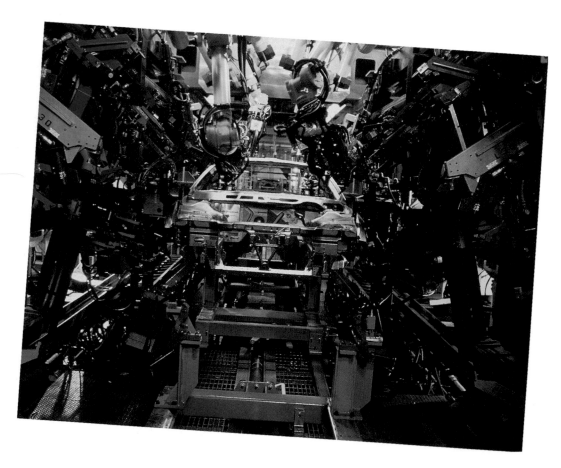

Car manufacturers use robotic assembly lines to build cars.

Programming

The future for programmers is very bright. As new computers and new uses are invented, there is a constant need for new programs. These careers are with the companies that build computers, those that write programs for computers, and with the millions of computer users.

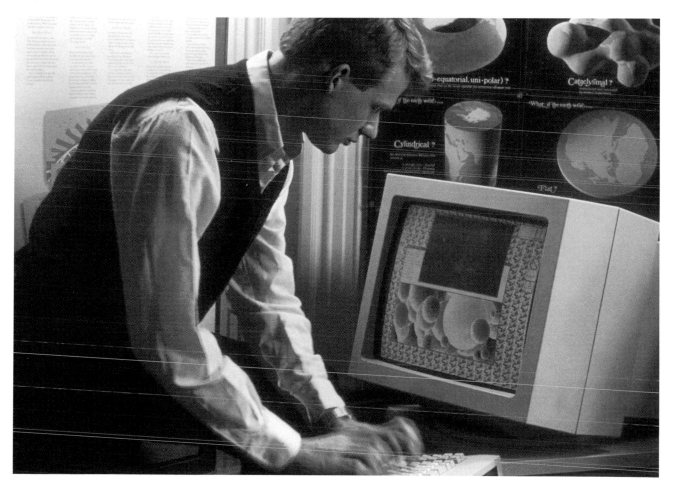

This program does tool modeling for NASA.

Graphic Design

By using modern computer technology, the graphic designers of the future will be creating exciting new designs in buildings, art, clothing, and dozens of other fields. Graphic designers will make extensive use of virtual reality to see how new designs look.

A computer-generated graphic.

Glossary

aircraft simulator—A box shaped like the nose of an airplane used to simulate conditions likely to occur in actual aircraft performance.

NASA—National Aeronautics and Space Administration. A federal agency set up by the U.S. Congress in 1958 to supervise U.S. space activities for peaceful purposes.

simulation—Imitation of the real situation.

space probes—Rocket-driven spacecraft used to explore space.

video conferencing—A way to hold a meeting using video cameras attached to a computer network.

virtual reality—Large computer program written to provide simulation.

Index

A

airplanes 4, 11, 19
airport 19
Apollo 13   7
astronauts 7, 9
automobiles 16, 23

B

bank robberies 19
baseball 21
buildings 15

C

classroom 13, 19, 21
college 21
computer design 25
computer display 13
computer programs 4, 16

D

deep-space probes 9
design 15, 19, 25, 26, 28
digital cameras 23
doctors 19
driver's test 16

E

Earth 10, 16
emergencies 7
environment 13
exams 19

F

factories 15
flight simulators 7
flight student 4
Florida 11
football 21
future 9, 13, 16, 24, 25, 27, 28

G

General Motors 15
gloves 13
graphic design 28

H

helmet 13
hockey 21
hurricanes 11

I

images 10
imitation 4
instrument panel 4, 6
interactive TV 21

J

Jupiter 9

L

laboratory experiments 21
launching pad 7
library 19

M

manufacturing 15, 26
meteors 10
moon 7
moon mission 7

N

NASA 7, 9, 10
Neptune 9

O

ocean 16
offices 15

P

passengers 7
personal computer 11
photography 23
pilots 4, 7
police officers 19
programming 27

R

race car 13
radio 19
radio signals 9, 10
rainstorm 11
real-life situations 16
robots 26

S

Saturn 9
school 16, 21
sensations 13
simulation 4, 7, 11
smells 13

Smithsonian Institute 10

snowstorm 11
sounds 13, 16
space 16
space program 7
space shuttle 7
space station 9
spacecraft 7, 9
sports 21
storms 11

T

telephone lines 19
television 11, 13, 19, 21, 23
tennis 21
tornadoes 11
traffic violations 19

U

Uranus 9

V

video conferencing 21
video games 13
virtual skills 10
Voyager 1 9
Voyager 2 9

W

Washington, D.C. 10
Weather Bureau, U.S. 11
weather forecasts 11
World Wide Web 21